Printed in Great Britain
by Amazon

52292286R00056